Captain

and the

Dog Star

Jonathan Emmett

Illustrated by Andy Parker

OXFORD

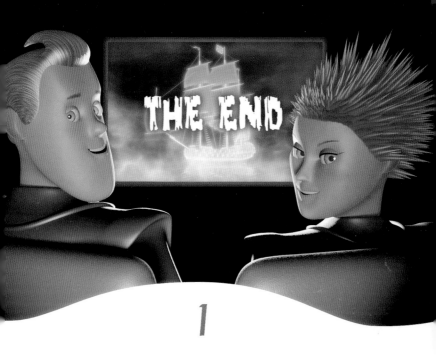

1

A ship in the night

It was midnight at Stardust Space
Station.

Captain Comet, Captain Stella and
Spanner the robot had been watching a
spooky film about a ghost ship.

'You can come out now, Spanner,'
said Captain Comet. 'The film has
finished.'

Spanner peeped out from under the lid of a rubbish bin. He looked very scared.

'Are ghost ships real?' he asked.

'Of course not, Spanner,' said Captain Stella, smiling.

Just then, the space scanner beeped.

'It's a spaceship,' said Comet, looking at the scanner screen. 'But it's just drifting.'

Captain Stella tried to talk to the spaceship on the video-link.

'This is Captain Stella of Stardust Space Station. Can you hear me?' she asked.

But there was no reply.

They could see the spaceship on the
video screen. It looked old and rusty.
The name *'Dog Star'* was painted on
its side.

'It looks like a ghost ship!'
gasped Spanner.

'It looks like space junk,' said
Comet. 'But we'd better check it out.'

Stella and Comet were getting into the space shuttle, when they noticed a bad smell. It was coming from an open hatch in the floor.

'Why is the rubbish hatch open?' Comet asked.

'Sorry,' said Spanner, 'I was supposed to empty the bins. I forgot.'

'Well, empty them now,' said Stella, 'and then close that hatch – someone could fall down it!'

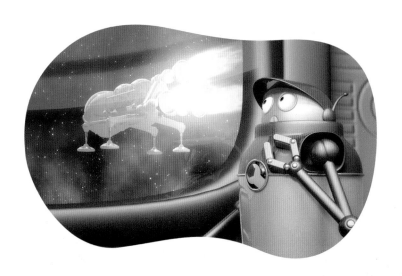

2

The Dog Star

Comet and Stella set off in the shuttle
and Spanner was left alone on the
space station. Spanner was still scared
after watching the spooky film. So he
went into Comet's cabin and hid under
the bedclothes. He forgot about
emptying the bins.

Comet docked the shuttle next to the *Dog Star*. Then he and Captain Stella pulled open the *Dog Star*'s entry door and climbed inside.

There were no lights on inside the old ship, so they used torches.

'There's no one here,' said Stella, looking around.

The inside of the ship was as scruffy as the outside. Everything was dirty and covered in dust.

'It's a bit spooky,' said Comet.

'Perhaps it is a *ghost ship* after all,' said Stella, smiling.

Comet and Stella found a flag
hanging at the front of the ship. It was
A SKULL AND CROSSBONES!
'Pirates!' gasped Stella.

Suddenly, there was a loud clang
from the back of the ship.

'That sounds like the entry door!'
said Stella.

They rushed back to see what was
happening and found the door closed.
Comet looked out of the window and
was shocked to see the shuttle leaving.

'We've been tricked!' groaned Comet.

3

Draco and Nova

Two space pirates, named Draco and
Nova, had stolen the shuttle.
The pirates had been hiding when
Comet and Stella had come on board.

'Nice ship,' said Draco, who was
flying the shuttle.

'Better than that old *Dog Star*,'
agreed Nova.

'Where are we going?' asked Draco, firing the shuttle's jets.

'Stardust Space Station,' said Nova, with an evil smile. 'There'll be no one there, so we can steal everything.'

Back on the space station, Spanner was still hiding under the bedclothes, wailing with fear. He was wailing so loudly that he didn't hear Comet's voice on the video-link.

'Spanner, this is Captain Comet calling. Spanner! Where are you?' said Comet's face on the video screen.

'Listen, the old spaceship is a trap. Space pirates have stolen the shuttle and are coming your way.'

Comet wondered why Spanner
didn't answer, but he went on, 'Don't let
the pirates on the space station! There's no fuel
in this ship, so we can't get back to help you.
You'll have to deal with them on your own.
Close all the doors and don't let them in.'

Comet looked worried.

'Spanner, can you hear me?'

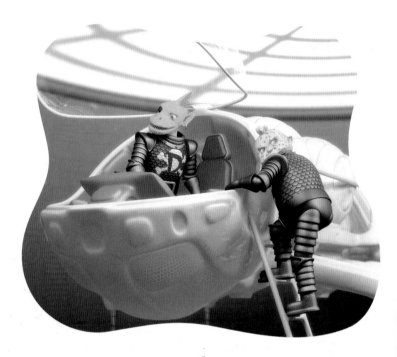

4

Spooky Spanner

But it was too late. The pirates had already landed inside the space station.

'What's that dreadful smell?' asked Draco, sniffing the air.

'It's coming from down there,' said Nova, pointing to the rubbish hatch.

'That needs closing – someone could fall down it,' said Draco.

The two pirates set off into the space station to see what they could steal.

They hadn't gone far before they heard a strange noise.

'What's that?' whispered Draco. 'It sounds like someone wailing.'

'I don't know,' said Nova. 'This station should only have two *humans* on it – and they're both on the *Dog Star*.'

'Perhaps it *isn't* human,' said Draco, nervously.

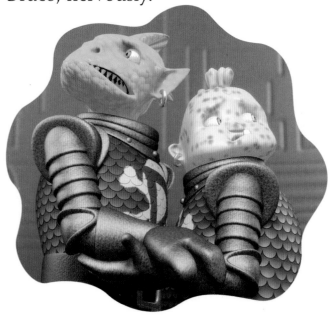

Spanner stopped wailing and heard the sound of footsteps coming towards him. 'Comet and Stella are back at last,' he thought.

At that moment, Draco and Nova entered the cabin. They saw Spanner get up, still covered in the bed sheet.

'A GHOST!' yelled the pirates.

'W-W-W-W-W-Where?' stammered Spanner.

22

Spanner pulled off the sheet, but the two scared pirates were already racing back to the shuttle. They were in such a hurry, they forgot about the open rubbish hatch.

'WHOA!' they moaned, as they both fell through it.

'URRGH!' they groaned, as they landed in the rubbish far below.

5

Comet comes back

Spanner was very scared. He had heard someone shouting about a ghost, but there was no one around. Then he heard a groaning sound. It was coming from the rubbish hatch.

'The ghost must be down there,' thought Spanner. He pressed the button quickly to close the hatch door.

It was only then that he heard Comet's voice on the video-link.

'Spanner,' said Comet, 'where have you been? I've been calling you for ages.'

Spanner picked up Comet and Stella in the shuttle. The robot was sure that there were no pirates on the space station – just a ghost. It was only when they got back and found Draco and Nova trapped down with the rubbish that they worked out what had happened.

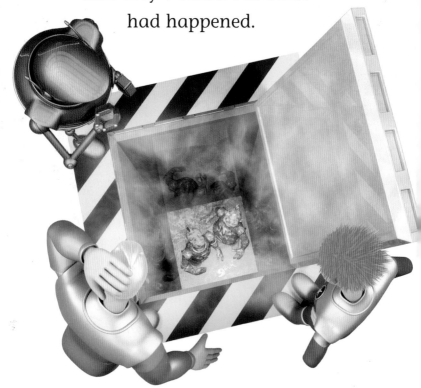

Draco and Nova were picked up
by a police ship and taken to a
prison planet.

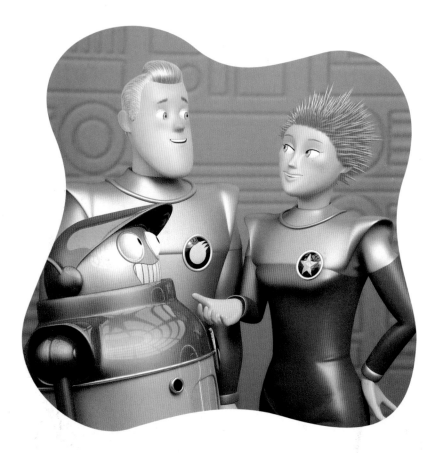

'That was a clever trick they played on us,' said Stella, when the pirates had gone.

'It was,' agreed Comet, 'but I bet they didn't feel so clever when they fell down that hatch.'

'Yes,' joked Spanner, 'they were clever at the start, but in the end they were *rubbish*!'

31

About the author

I got the idea for this story while I was writing my first Captain Comet book.
I thought that it must be very quiet and lonely on a space station, with nobody to talk to for thousands of miles. It's just the sort of place where you might start to imagine things that aren't really there.

You can find out more about Jonathan Emmett's books by visiting his website at www.scribblestreet.co.uk